The Handbook of Urban Druidry

Modern Druidry for All

The Handbook
of Urban Druidry

Modern Druidry for All

Brendan Howlin

Winchester, UK
Washington, USA

First published by Moon Books, 2014
Moon Books is an imprint of John Hunt Publishing Ltd., Laurel House, Station Approach,
Alresford, Hants, SO24 9JH, UK
office1@jhpbooks.net
www.johnhuntpublishing.com
www.moon-books.net

For distributor details and how to order please visit the 'Ordering' section on our website.

Text copyright: Brendan Howlin 2013

ISBN: 978 1 78279 376 2

A CIP catalogue record for this book is available from the British Library.

Design: Lee Nash

Printed and bound by CPI Group (UK) Ltd, Croydon, CR0 4YY

We operate a distinctive and ethical publishing philosophy in all
areas of our business, from our global network of authors to
production and worldwide distribution.

CONTENTS

An excellent down-to-earth and witty introduction to how Druidry can help us in the 21st century.
Philip Carr-Gomm

For Gillian, my wife and my light, love and inspiration.

Acknowledgements

Thanks are owing to many people for this book. Principally, to my Bardic and Ovate tutees over the years whose questions have formed my ideas, many of whom are now firm friends, particularly Anthony and Rosemary, Ray Stirton and Jan Nolan. Thanks to my friends in OBOD for their unstinting friendship and support, particularly Fiona Ware, Karen James, Marion Sibbons, Shaun Hayes, Anne MacDonald Coleman, Susan Jones and Penny Billington. My colleagues in my 'real' life who make lunchtime and coffee enjoyable, particularly Anna Tanczos, Michael Pounds and Ian Hamerton. My special thanks to my family for providing support by just being there and finally to Philip Carr-Gomm who put us all on this path in the first place. Lastly, a special mention to Stuart Lythgoe for starting this idea off many years ago.

Incidentally, if you enjoy this book and practise some of the ideas or have ideas of your own then please let me know on urbandruid1@gmail.com. I will collect the best ideas and promote them on my website.

Introduction

Have you ever thought that there must be a better way to live than the way you do now? Do you feel that you are a helpless pawn in your own life, a life that is increasingly out of your control? Do you feel stressed and tired all the time trying to cope with the demands of your life and never having enough time for yourself?

If you do then you are not alone, these feelings are extremely common and there is a way out. In this book I will tell you about a way that works, it is called Urban Druidry. What, I hear you ask, is Urban Druidry? Aren't Druids funny old men and women who dress up in white robes and hang around Stonehenge at the summer solstice? How on earth can that be relevant to me and my life? The answer is Druidry is not about wearing a white robe, the underlying philosophy can be practised by anyone, of any religious persuasion and great benefits can accrue in anyone's life.

If you have heard anything about Druidry you will know that is a nature-based way of life, so how is this relevant to people who live in cities? Read on and you will learn about living Druidry in the heart of a modern city without a requirement for a single grove of Oak trees to be present. The best part of Druidry is that there is no dogma, there is no requirement to follow any of the precepts or ideals; you make up your own mind and do things your way. Hence it is a most adaptable way of life and is able to satisfy a wide variety of people and their lifestyles. So read on and find out what works for you. In essence even if you just recognise the problems that you have in your life you will have succeeded.

The beauty of Druidry is that it does not stipulate a

religious belief. You are free to frame your concept of Deity in whatever way suits you. Hence I know of Christian Druids, Buddhist Druids, Pagan Druids, Secular Druids and even one Sufi Druid. In this confused modern age, a way of life that respects difference is most important. Druids share a common practice not a common set of beliefs, so the Druid who stands next to me may believe entirely different things to me but we can still stand together in tolerance and understanding.

This book is organised in sections, it works best if you follow the structure and do each section in turn because you are trying to change your preconceptions and expectations about life, and each section will build on the next. Part 1 is basically a self-help course designed to be followed for a year and a day that will introduce you experientially to the basics of Urban Druidry. The second part will relate what you have learned to 'real' Druidry.

Part 1

First Things First

Chapter 1

Learning to See

We will start with the single most important aspect of this book and it will be unexpected. If you do this first section, your life will change beyond your expectations and it is easily within everyone's power. The first section is the seemingly trivial advice to learn to see. This might sound crazy to you, as most people can already see quite well, otherwise they would have difficulty in getting about, but believe me most people are hardly aware of their environment and what is going on around them.

I have stood at the window of my flat and looked out at the car park. It was about 5:30 on an autumn afternoon and people were coming and going to their cars. Standing in the car park as bold a brass was a large fox and everyone walked by it as if it wasn't there. The people were so wrapped up in their own thoughts and concerns that they just didn't see. You would be surprised to learn that this situation happens all the time in most people's lives. Obviously, it is not a fox that they miss all the time otherwise the country would be overrun with foxes, but there are many, many examples of people not seeing what is in front of their noses because they won't see. Not because they can't but because they won't.

If we take another example, most people can remember their childhood. Some can't, so if you are one of these then don't worry, we are in the same boat. When you are a child the world is a magical place, everything is a delight. The world is magical because you haven't much experience of it, but also because you are in the moment. You aren't beset with worries and cares that take your attention away from what is happening right now in front of you. Most people will also say that being a child was a happy carefree time but you lose that feeling when you become an adult.

Obviously you can't go back to the freedom of childhood, where you can run about as much as you like knowing that if you get tired your father or mother will pick you up, feed you and put you to bed. We really don't appreciate how well off we were when we were kids. This is because we have no sense of personal responsibility; the responsibility is all given over to your parents. So how do we go about recapturing some of this magic? The answer is to learn to see.

You will probably say that you don't have time to spend staring at things in your busy day and this is probably true, but even the busiest of us can learn to see more during our days. If you go to work by car, you have the time that you walk to the car and from the car to work to see. This may be only a few minutes, but if you learn to see in this time you will already have accomplished something. You will probably also say what can I see? I live in a housing estate with concrete all around me, what is there to see that I haven't seen before? Strangely enough even the most urban of environments is teeming with life, which I will expand on later but even without this there is still the sky. The sky, you say, I've seen that, I see it every day. I know that, but have you looked! Whenever I travel by train I always sit by a window and look out. I have noticed on a busy commuter train from London in the evening that when I am looking out and seeing a truly remarkable glorious red sunset everyone else has their noses in books, newspapers or laptops and isn't seeing it. Why not? It is wonderful and it is free. There can't be one person who isn't moved by a spectacular sunset and there are many of these every year. This is just one example of what we can see if we actually look.

If you travel to work by car you will have a minute or two when you are walking from your house to your car and another minute or two when you arrive at your destination to use for seeing. Obviously you should confine your seeing when you are driving to the driving, but otherwise look. I cannot recommend too highly a book by Gavin Pretor-Pinney called *The Cloudspotter's Guide*, which tells you about the different types of clouds in an amusing and interesting way. Armed with the information in this book you will be able to classify even the most mundane of skyscapes. Looking up at the sky has other important benefits, such as knowing if it is going to rain or not, but also has important psychological benefits. When we are upset we say we are downcast or just down, so the mere act of looking up cheers you up. Our language is very instructive if we pay attention to how we use it.

If you take the time to look, even if it is only twice a day in the car driving exercise, you have increased the amount of time for yourself in your day. This instantly makes your day feel longer and fuller and you feel like you are getting something out of it for yourself. If you do this often you will look forward to your seeing time and you will have already made a big step towards both Urban Druidry and enlightenment.

If you do look at the sky you cannot fail to see birds, they will cross your field of vision all the time. There are a surprising number and variety of birds in even the most urban of environments and they are interesting. Again, like in our cloud example, if you look you will soon want to know a bit more about them, what the different species are, etc. There are a huge variety of bird spotting manuals and field guides available and you don't have to go the whole way and become a twitcher, but a little knowledge helps. It helps in a large number of ways but one side benefit is that as we get older we tend to close down and not take things in as much. There is a lot of evidence now that learning new things and keeping your interest up may help prevent you suffering from senility, etc. The old adage, use it or lose it, is very true.

I taught a student of mine the sounds of common birds, like blackbird, dove, etc. and she was chuffed when she was the only person amongst her peers who could answer a set of questions on University Challenge on common bird sounds, so there are unexpected benefits too, like impressing your friends.

Inevitably in a book about Druidry I am going to mention trees. There are trees everywhere in an urban environment, a lot of which may well be foreign trees but this doesn't matter. In London the stately London plane trees are always a delight with their patchwork bark and large green leaves and those funny spiky ball-like seed pods. In other places you will see many species. In the UK, the Woodland Trust produces a nice swatch book that helps you identify native species, but it doesn't matter if you know species and type as long as you know your tree or trees. The one you pass going to work every day will become a friend if you actually notice it. Trees are living beings, they grow, they breathe and they can suffer too. It enrages me when I hear of people cutting down trees because the sap is marking their cars. Trees play a vital role in dealing with the carbon dioxide that we produce through driving cars, using central heating, etc. and I don't know of one person who actually doesn't like looking at them. Treat them with respect. Respect is something that we will be coming back to later as it is very important in Urban Druidry but I mention it here to flag it up.

I count myself extremely lucky in that I can walk to work

every day. OK, when it is pouring with rain for day after day, I don't feel quite so lucky but in general I am. I get to walk down the High Street and see the trees on the top of the North Downs framed by the street. I walk across a footbridge over a river and get to see the moods of the river over the year, from the slow thick flow of the winter to the quick brown spring flow. I get to see lots of trees. I see them come into leaf in the spring with that fresh green colour of early spring and lose their leaves in the autumn. I see birds. I see the swifts arrive in the early summer and see flocks of migrating geese in the autumn and all this in a town that is literally choked with traffic.

So take the opportunity to look around you and notice what you see, it will enrich your life, you will see more and more things that you have never noticed before and you will become aware of the web of life flowering around you. Ideally you should observe your environment over a year and take note of the changes that you see happening because next time round they will be like old friends to you that you are meeting again. It also impresses your workmates if you can say, 'The willows are looking particularly nice this year'. So wake up and look around you, don't let the beauty of life pass you by. The reason we are on this earth must be to experience what is here, so it is never too late to start doing it and benefiting from it.

One added advantage of seeing what is around you is that it distracts you. If you notice what is around you, you can't walk along brooding about how mean your boss is to you or how awful your job is. This is extremely valuable because obsession is the enemy of enlightenment. When you are spending every minute of the day turning over your problems in your mind, you are not living in the present and thereby wasting your life. If you see Buddhist monks they are always smiling and laughing because life is good and is meant to be enjoyed. This is also the key to the Buddhist philosophy of forgiving your enemies. This does not mean forget what they have done to you, it simply means don't brood on your grievance all the time and think about what you can do to get back at them. If you do this your enemy has power over you all of the time. You can be certain that your enemy is not thinking about you (probably not at all actually) so why are you thinking about them? So when you allow yourself to become distracted by an interesting cloud, or tree or bird you have broken this cycle and can then be said to have forgiven your enemies.

There is unfortunately a distraction that heterosexual men indulge in that can also not be beneficial. I speak here only of heterosexual men because that is what I know best, if this applies to gay unions as well then great. Heterosexual men like to indulge in bird spotting of the non-feathered kind. This is perfectly natural and no harm at all except when it leads to dissatisfaction. If you are constantly feeling a lack because your partner isn't as good as those that you are spotting then there is something wrong. You are stressing yourself instead of relaxing your mind and allowing yourself to be present. This is a signal to sort out your life and if anything becomes an obsession then it is harmful to your pursuit of Urban Druidry.

I hope I have shown you how to break the cycle of stress that you find yourself in and make a start on the path to Urban Druidry. My advice about seeing applies equally well to the other senses too. Our other senses are equally as dulled by our lifestyles and if you reawaken them then your quality of life will improve. Women generally tend to be much better at appreciating the other senses. I used to use nasal inhalers quite often and had lost my sense of smell, but when I stopped I was amazed at how much my sense of smell improved. I joked to my wife that I smell just like a woman now but she told me that would only be true if I had a bath! The only proviso to this advice is to be careful with the sense of touch. There are very strong restrictions and taboos about touching in society so be sensible. Also I cut my hand open touching a plant in South Africa, which actually had very sharp leaves and I didn't know this, so please use some discretion.

The sense of hearing can be a problem with men in relationships. We often tend to suffer from what is termed spousal deafness after a while in a relationship. Understandably this is very upsetting to our partners. If your partner whispers 'let's have sex now' most men will probably hear but if she shouts 'take out the rubbish bins' we won't. The origin of this is obvious and relates to our own dissatisfaction and selfishness. It is probably why many older men end up suffering from hearing problems because it becomes a habit after a while, so it is important to acknowledge this and try to listen more carefully. The reward will be a happier partner and a better life.

Summary

1. Learn to see
2. Take time to look around you and notice your environment.
3. Take time to pause before getting in the car.
4. Notice the birds, flowers and trees around you.
5. Stop obsessing about how hard done by you are.
6. Start living in the here and now.

Chapter 2

Learning to Relax

So after you have been seeing for a while what then? The next step on the path of Urban Druidry is to learn to relax. It is appalling that this is the one thing that most of us have forgotten how to do, even if we ever knew how to. As mentioned above obsession is an enemy of enlightenment; so is stress. This is not to say that every Urban Druid is always going to be serene and smiling. Of course not, life is too genuinely stressful for that but you can go a long way towards reducing the unnecessary stress. Many of us, if the truth is known, are addicted to a little bit of stress in our lives as it adds a bit of a frisson that we wouldn't have otherwise. However, we hear a lot about toxic stress these days and this has to be wrong.

When we have learnt to see we have reduced some of the stress in our lives, but how do we proceed? We need to identify the things that stress us and seek to reduce or modify them. Technology is one of the major stress objects in our lives and television and mobile phones are two of the greatest. Mobile phones are easier to understand. If someone can reach you whenever they want then they will and note it is when they want and not when you want. I have heard people say that they can switch off their phones when they don't want to be disturbed but there is no point in having the phone if it is always switched off. Mobile phones also mitigate against seeing. I frequently see people walking along apparently talking to themselves and I am sure that they are not taking in their surroundings. I am surprised that many of them don't get mugged or run over. Don't get me wrong, there are many situations where mobile phones are extremely useful; it is overuse of them that causes stress.

Many people like to enliven the boredom of going to work every day by playing music. There is nothing wrong in this and it may even cheer you up. The danger is playing your iPod (or whatever) all the time and using it as a way to avoid thinking about what you are doing or what is actually concerning you. This is called not being in the moment. We all like escapism and there is a definite role for this in life but not to the exclusion of actually living your life. How are you going to hear the birds singing or that run away juggernaut bearing down on you? Some kinds of music are actually designed to stress you, as I will discuss later, so it may not be a good idea to listen to these kinds of music before that important meeting with the boss.

Likewise, the humble television, which is a source of company to many lonely people, is also a major source of stress. If you absolutely have to see a particular programme at a certain time, it stresses you. The television schedule is your master, not you its. Also advertising on television is designed to stress you, to make you feel a lack. I know the advertising agencies say that they can't force you to buy anything, just suggest alternatives, but nevertheless advertising creates images that you want to conform to. Happy, contented people don't go out shopping to fill a hole in themselves. So, I'm not saying don't ever watch the evil television again, just be aware of what you are doing and why. I quite like to watch films on the telly but find that my mind is so active sometimes afterwards that I can't sleep, so I get tired and stressed.

One startling fact is that if you don't switch on your television you don't miss it after a while, you always have the power to turn it off. So try reducing your dependency on television, you will be the healthier and calmer for it.

OK, so now you've got a lot more time from not watching the telly, what do you do? Breathing exercises and meditation are great things to do to relax and don't have to take long.

Most of us have forgotten how to breathe, which sounds stupid because we'd all be dead but I mean forgotten how to breathe properly. A proper breath is deep from the diaphragm not shallowly from the chest. This short breathing is caused by stress. You have probably noticed yourself that when you get stressed you tend to breathe faster and shallower. This kind of breathing becomes a habit after a while and you forget that you are doing it. A consequence of this is that you become tolerant to a higher level of carbon dioxide in your body and there is some evidence that asthmatics in particular have become habituated to this. One simple thing that you can do to change this is to breathe out more than you breathe in. This relaxes you automatically; you don't have to do anything else. The next thing to try is to do a few deep breaths every morning or evening. Breathe in through your nose for a count of four, hold your breath without straining for another count of four and then breathe out by contracting your stomach and diaphragm. When your breath is out, lower your diaphragm to fill your lungs again. Repeat this nine or ten times a day and you will be surprised at the change in your energy levels. A side effect of this is that it gives your stomach and intestine a good workout and can help with digestive problems as well.

Now comes meditation and there is a lot of misunderstanding about meditation. To be honest a proper study of it would take a great deal more space than this book takes up, but it is not my intention to make you an expert in anything, just to introduce simple things that you can do to improve your life and as a side effect make you an

Urban Druid.

Meditation is basically sitting quietly not thinking of anything, it is that simple. The key to it and the main benefits that it produces are: a) some time for yourself when you aren't doing anything and b) just as in learning to see above, it breaks the cycle of obsessive thinking and worrying. Both of these activities are extremely difficult for stressed people to do, so if you can actually succeed in both of these endeavours you have automatically lessened your level of stress. It is astonishing how many people just cannot bear to be alone with themselves and their thoughts. If you are one of these people then there is obviously something wrong with your life. We use all sorts of displacement activities to avoid being alone, e.g. television and mobile phones as mentioned above. These activities also include drinking alcohol, smoking, playing computer games, etc.

Now meditation isn't something that has to be done for hours or even done outside in a nice woodland setting, it can be done for just five minutes a day in your own lounge or bedroom. In practice it is also not advisable to meditate for a long time until you are more balanced in your life. There is an adage that says people are crazy anyway and too much meditation makes them crazier.

So how is it done? Well first of all you have to find somewhere comfortable to sit where you won't be disturbed for at least five minutes. You don't have to invest in expensive clothing or meditation cushions, unless you really want to. Just wear something that doesn't restrict your breathing too much. You don't even have to sit cross-legged if you don't want to. In practice many men find this difficult to do anyway and unless you are flexible it might hurt and then the pain will distract you from the benefits. The most important thing is to be comfortable and to be able to sit up straight.

When you are sitting comfortably (like Listen with Mother if you are British and of a certain age!) then take a few deep breaths in the way that we discussed earlier. Close your eyes so that you can't see anything going on around you as this will just distract you. This is incidentally why you need to find a safe place where you are not going to be disturbed. Someone sneaking up on you when your eyes are closed can be quite distracting if not shocking. The same thing applies to pet animals; a cat leaping into your lap can also break your concentration. Also, if you don't feel safe, you won't be able to relax and if you aren't able to relax, you can't meditate. When you are settled, concentrate on your breathing, just observing it coming in and going out and try not to think of anything. If any thoughts do appear just imagine pushing them away until your mind is still and calm. You won't be able to do this every time because there will be times when you won't be able to calm your mind or some distraction becomes too great to ignore. If this happens don't force it, just try again the next day. The important thing is to find some benefit from this, not to make another rod to beat yourself up with. When your mind is calm you will notice that your breathing is getting slower and you don't need to breathe quite as often.

With practice your breathing will slow and time will seem to dilate for you. This is why five minutes a day is good, because five minutes of good meditation will feel like an incredibly long time. If you can sit calmly for just five minutes a day you will again have added more time for yourself into your lifestyle, i.e. more 'me' time and your day will seem longer and fuller. You will also have broken the cycle of concentrating on your worries again and will feel happier.

During this process you will inevitably have found out what worries you most, as these will be the thoughts that you get most often when you are trying to clear your mind. Therefore, if it is in your power, you can take steps to reduce or eliminate these problems and worries. You will have learned a lot about yourself and also learned to deal with what bothers you. So even if you don't manage to meditate you will still have gained a lot.

If you do learn to meditate you will find that things which once seemed extremely important aren't now and life will be better. Many people like to listen to music when they are meditating and this is really up to you. I often find it distracting and prefer to have absolute quiet, but obviously some kinds of music are better than others for meditation. Rock music generally isn't, because the objective of rock music is to stir you up and excite you, so it doesn't help meditation. Quieter music is generally better, like classical or New Age music. However, all people are different and I know of some people who do meditate to rock music and enjoy it. People tend to get distressed when they read things like this, which offer lots of alternatives, but the point is that you must find what works for you and that means making decisions. Many people do all they can to avoid making decisions and this inevitably leads to stress. If you don't know what you want, you are always at the beck and call of someone else and this is not good. Making decisions is called personal responsibility and is also a central tenet of Urban Druidry, but we will come to this later.

By this stage you will have learned to see and observe what is going on around you. You will have learned to breathe and meditate and take life a bit easier, so will have relaxed a great deal. Hopefully you will have broken the obsessional cycle that you may have found yourself in, you will be calmer and less worried about what life has to throw at you and are now ready to move on to the advanced stuff.

Summary

1. Learn to relax
2. Reduce your dependence on your mobile phone.
3. Try turning your television off.
4. Learn to breathe properly.
5. Take 5 minutes a day to meditate.

Chapter 3

Getting in Tune with the Seasons

The advanced stuff naturally builds on what you have already learnt, which is how a structured course works. The next stage is to get back in tune with the seasons and the rhythm of life. I know this sounds like 'really hippy stuff man', but it is another facet of our lives that we have lost. Our 24/7 lives have left us feeling dislocated and distressed and we will all be a great deal happier if we can return to a semi-natural state.

This sounds really complicated, but what it means is to extend your seeing to the time period of one whole year. Humans are naturally part of the whole cycle of life on this planet and we evolved (if you believe in evolution) to be in tune with the earth and its rhythms. A good example of this is the feeling you get in winter, when it is cold and dark and you just want to curl up in front of a warm fire and snooze. I call this the hibernation instinct. I know humans can't hibernate as we would die of starvation, but it is a good working description. Likewise in the height of summer, you feel like running about and doing things (if it is not too hot, which if you are in the UK it is unlikely to be often). These feelings are just you responding to the rhythms of the seasons. Naturally it is not a good idea to run about and be creative in six feet of snow nor is it a good idea to snooze in the sun in the height of summer, as you could suffer badly from sunburn. So the point of this is to become aware of the passing of the seasons by observing what is happening around you and responding to how you feel at the time.

When you observe over a year, you will see the leaves

turn brown and fall off in the autumn, you will see the stark bare winter branches and you will have a little thrill when you see the new leaves appear in spring. Finally at the height of summer when everything is full blown you will feel the onset of decay and the start of the decline to autumn and winter again. This is another way to impress your friends and colleagues as they probably won't have noticed this happening but also if you do this you will start to feel part of life again. This is a subtle feeling but well worth cultivating because being out of kilter with the seasons also causes stress. OK, you can't take every day off work and sleep in the winter even if you wanted to. You just have to take things easier in the winter, acknowledge that you feel like sleeping more and doing things more slowly and follow that feeling. If you take things easier in the winter you will build up your reserves and both feel like, and be able to, do more in the summer.

There seems to be some evidence that most people are sleep deprived. This is a consequence of our 24-hour lifestyle, so it is important to get enough sleep. Sleep is vitally important for your mental health and your energy levels. Too little sleep can be extremely damaging to both of these. I remember reading about a sleep study, where people were put in a unit for a week and told to sleep as much as they liked. On the first day most of them slept for 14 hours, but by the end of the week they had reverted to a 'normal' 7 or 8 hours. The conclusion from this is that initially people are paying off their sleep debt and once that is paid off, a normal sleeping pattern ensues. Therefore the lifestyles that they normally live are leaving them tired with not enough sleep.

By now you will have realised that walking is probably the best way to do your observation and again it can be done in short sections. The important thing is to take the time to observe what is happening in the natural world around you even if only for 5 minutes. So you don't have to go for marathon walks every day, you could just observe the same tree or bush, but the important thing is to do it. However, don't choose an evergreen bush because you could be waiting a long time for something to happen!

Summary

1. Get in tune with the seasons.
2. Observe a whole year passing.
3. Get enough sleep.
4. Take short walks to get to 'feel' the time of the year.
5. Select a tree and watch it change over the year.

Chapter 4

Living the Wheel of the Year

'Real Druids' get in tune with the seasons by celebrating eight seasonal festivals in the year, each roughly one-and-a-half months apart. They are based around the four fire festivals and the two solstices and two equinoxes. Almost everyone has heard about Druids meeting at Stonehenge to celebrate the summer solstice and most people know this occurs at about the 21st June.

I have presented one form of the wheel of the year in the diagram, so that you can see how it works and what each part is called.

The Wheel of the Year

1st August ———→ 21st September

Lugnasadh

Autumn Equinox

21st June

31st October

Summer Solstice

Samhain (Halloween)

Beltane (May Day)

Alban Arthan (Christmas)

21st December

1st May

Spring Equinox

Imbolc

21st March ←——— 1st February

The important point is that each festival follows the one before in an endlessly repeating cycle and this cycle also follows the cycle of the seasons and therefore the cycle of nature. As creatures of nature we are also in tune with the seasons and the growing and fading of light so this scheme offers one way to acknowledge this and turn it to our advantage in practising Urban Druidry.

The Summer Solstice – Maximum Creativity

The summer solstice is when the hours of daylight are at their largest (the longest day) and naturally you feel like taking maximum advantage of this, so creativity and power are at their heights. Druids are concerned with something that is called Awen, which is a Welsh word meaning creativity and to make this easier to understand, it just means getting more out of life by being creative.

We all remember the joy that we felt as kids when we built model aeroplanes or made clothes for our dolls. Kids are eternally creative, forever drawing, painting, making up games and what's more important they have a lot of fun too.

Obviously we can't go back to being kids again but we can recapture some of that joy in life by giving rein to our creativity. All that means is doing something you enjoy. Almost everyone has a hobby of some kind and it provides an area of peace and fulfilment in the day. If you are a couch potato and don't have any hobbies maybe you should think about getting one. It doesn't have to be expensive or require a great deal of costly kit or even require a lot of time. If you spend time doing something that you enjoy you will feel better about life. We get depressed when we feel that there isn't anything for us in our days, we are working for someone else and maybe looking after the kids in the evening. A hobby gives you that magical 'me' time and allows you to look back and say 'I accomplished something today'.

The key to Awen and thereby Urban Druidry is doing what is right for you and this means the hobby that is truly what you want to do. How do you know whether you are doing what is right for you? Take for example, practising the violin because Aunty Sue said you were good though actually you hate it. In this particular case you probably already know that what you should do is not play the violin and find something else to do immediately, but the general point is still valid.

One big problem we all have these days is choice. How do you work out what you want to do when there is a bewildering array of activities out there? In the past when we all worked on the land the only leisure choices were lazing around or drinking in the pub, so the question of choice never really entered in to it. The sheer variety of possibilities can be pretty daunting these days. How do you know that you really want to do bungee jumping for instance? This brings me naturally to the problem of choice. A lot of people actually find choice difficult and would prefer to be told what to do. If you find yourself in this category then the solution is easy… join a group!

Really it is not too much of a problem finding out if you enjoy something or not, just try it. You will soon find out if you have an aptitude for it or not and if you haven't then just try something else. In the worst case you will be a bit of a nomad for a while but to use management speak you will be building up your skills base.

One word of warning here, there is a tendency that is especially apparent in 'New Agers' to flit like a butterfly from one activity to another and never achieve much. If you talk to these people they have tried everything, but only did Tai Chi for three months, etc. Some activities require a decent length of time to be committed to them in order to reap the benefits, so it is worth persevering even if you find that the first few lessons, or attempts, aren't that useful. Of course if you absolutely hate what you are doing then leave immediately. Your body and mind often know exactly what is good or bad for you and if you learn to listen to them, then you will be the happier for it.

If you do find what you want to do then you will feel fulfilled and much happier and it will have been well worth all the effort.

Summary

1. Find time to do something that you really want to do.

Lugnasadh – What Can You Finish?

If we count from the summer solstice, the next festival is one-and-a-half months later, i.e. the start of August and this is traditionally called Lugnasadh (or Lammas) or to make it easier the start of harvest. At this time the days have started to get shorter and it is common to feel a sense of completion, i.e. a feeling of finishing things and taking things a bit easier.

This is a good time to take stock and lay things in for the winter as you will see squirrels doing if you look out of your window (remember keep looking and seeing!).

One frequent complaint about modern life and modern work in particular is that there is never a sense of completion. You work hard and clear your desk and the reward is another load of work. It is difficult to achieve a sense of completion and of a job well done. If you add to this modern management systems where you are working for someone who hasn't the faintest idea what you do and probably doesn't care anyway as long as they get their salary, then you may never get the feeling that you are appreciated and cared for. Another facet of the modern world is the constant threat of redundancy, which the Government likes to call flexible working practices, and this is not designed to make you feel secure. I have a theory that companies work better when everyone knows everyone else and they all feel that they are involved in the end product, whatever that may be. As soon as the company grows above this size then disaffection sets in and workers become 'jobsworths' and don't really care about the output (but I'm not a management consultant, so what do I know?). I appreciate that your situation may not be like this but there are many cases that are. So now is the time to look at yourself and your life and see what hanging threads there are, for example the redecoration of the bathroom that you have been putting off, then get on and do it. You know you will feel much better and you won't have that hanging over your head any longer. There is also the additional advantage that if your partner has been nagging you to get something done, then you can hold your head up and say, 'It's done!'.

Summary

1. Find something to complete.

The Autumn Equinox – What Have You Achieved?

One-and-a-half months from Lugnasadh takes us to mid September, which is the autumn equinox (which is the time of equal day and night). By this time the harvest was traditionally gathered in and people were basking in a feeling of a job well done and wanting to relax a bit. The summer is over and autumn is beginning, so it is natural to look back on what you have achieved in the year.

There is a theory that one of the reasons for the end of our life on this earth is because we have stored so much information that there is no room for any more, so the secret of a long life is to take time regularly to process what we have done and let go of any extraneous information. The autumn equinox is a good time to do this, as the mellow feeling that you have at this time helps beneficial reflexion. Obviously this process isn't that beneficial if you review what you have done and end up with lots of discouraging and dispiriting events and thereby decrease your sense of self worth. However, even if you do feel like this to a certain extent the process is still beneficial if you can learn from the events. You would be surprised (or maybe not) at how we resist learning from events in our lives. I often think that the self destructive urge is very strong in all of us and this coupled with our mulish (maybe unfair to mules here!) egos stop us moving on. So if on reflexion you find some events that you are not too proud of (and to be honest how many of us can say otherwise) then treat it (them) as things that you can avoid next time by changing your behaviour. Getting on my hobby horse again, it is incredible how many people think that they can't change their behaviour when all the evidence points to people constantly changing their behaviour throughout life. This urge for constancy and lack of change is something that I have mentioned before but it's worth stressing it.

Of course the best thing to do is to review what has happened in the past year, find some things that you have done well and congratulate yourself. Next find some things that you haven't done so well and resolve to try to do things differently next time and forgive yourself, then look forward to another exciting, challenging year.

Summary

1. Take time to bask in the feeling of a 'job well done'.

Halloween – Proper Grieving

The next festival is at the end of October, traditionally called Halloween, which is the start of winter. This festival seems to have become quite popular in recent times, with people wanting to dress up and have a bit of a party. This was the end of the Celtic year, as darkness closed in on the land and no work could be done in the fields until next year. It was a time to honour the dead, those who had gone on, and to stay indoors out of the weather. The whole subject of death is one that we try to avoid in our youth-culture-based modern lifestyle. We fear getting old, not being competitive any more, losing our faculties, etc. This is also tied up with modern parenting and parents wanting to be 'cool', but this is a whole other subject and another book. In fact it is one, it is called *The Madness of Modern Families* by Annie Ashworth and Meg Sanders. This is a fantastic book and very funny and if you are a parent and can identify yourself in it, so much the better.

Of course, it is a law of psychology that something that is buried always comes out somewhere else and the preoccupation of our entertainment with murder, forensics and horror is that other side. Far better then to acknowledge what is after all the only inevitable fact of life, the fact that we all must die, and deal with it. As far as I know Buddhists are very good at this and contemplating a good death is regularly practised by them. However, we are not all Buddhists or even very good, so Halloween is a good time to think on this. Remember your loved ones who have passed on, remember their lives, their sayings, your feelings about them. This is called honouring the dead. I believe that in Mexico they have parties in graveyards on the graves of their departed and spend some time with them. I don't advocate this here as for one reason the weather is often pretty dodgy at Halloween and also you might get picked up by the police if they see lights and hear music coming from the local graveyard.

If you do remember the departed in this way then in essence they don't die because they live on in our hearts and minds and you can hope that someone will do the same for you when you go. This is a sneaky exhortation to live a good life, as then there will be things that others will find worth remembering from your life.

Summary

1. Take time to remember the departed.

Alban Arthan – Celebration

The next festival in the calendar is called Alban Arthan in Druidry but most people would recognise it as Christmas. At this time it has been dark and cold for a while but it is the time of the winter solstice, where the earth has reached its maximum distance from the sun and is turning around in its elliptical orbit to come closer again. This is why Druids call it the return of the light because even if you can't see it, the long nights of winter are over and the days will start to lengthen. People have always felt like celebrating at this time with good food, presents, etc. It is also a time when we feel like being with our families. The ancient Romans also had a special festival at this time of the year, called Saturnalia, where people enjoyed themselves in a variety of ways, not unlike our current Christmas celebrations.

In Surrey on Boxing Day, a strange spontaneous custom takes place. Many local people in Surrey are seized by the desire to walk up the hill to St. Martha's Church, just outside Guildford. If you ask them why they are doing it you get a variety of answers, the most common being that they felt the need to walk off the excesses of Christmas day. If you have never been there, St. Martha's is an odd church, as it is perched on the top of a hill with no water supply. If you believe in earth power then you will feel it strongly at the top of St. Martha's hill and if you don't then you will just feel happier and more relaxed somehow. Records speak of a number of Druid circles on the hill and the church was obviously put there to focus attention on what they thought people should be feeling. Interestingly the first thing you see when you enter the church is a painting of St. George killing the dragon, which is symbolic of Christianity taming the earth power represented as a dragon. Also there is apparently no St. Martha who is supposed to be commemorated by the building of the church. If you look further you will find that it is supposed to be a corruption of martyrs, but no one knows which martyrs are being referred to. So this is a perfect example of people unconsciously getting in tune with the seasons and getting out to top up their earth energy. This has obviously been going on for a long time, perhaps even from pre-Christian times. Of course the view from the top of the hill is wonderful, so it is well worth a visit even if you don't believe any of this. I am sure there are lots of places and customs like this that are widespread over whatever country you are in. You could argue that this is not an example of Urban Druidry as I am talking about walking in the country, but St. Martha's is less than half an hour's walk from Guildford High Street. It doesn't matter if you don't go out in the country, just find the celebration that suits you.

Incidentally this is the time that many people decide on

New Year's resolutions and resolve to do something different in the coming year. You may also have noticed how many of these resolutions have fallen by the wayside in a very short time. This is due in part to inertia (it is very difficult to change your lifestyle and/or behaviour if both your heart and soul aren't in it) and partly to sheer laziness (which to be honest we all suffer from at some time). There is also a Druidic reason for this and it is that this is the wrong time of the year for this. The New Year as we have it is a somewhat artificial concept and it never really feels different on January the First (apart for the lack of sleep and/or the monumental hangover!). The real time for starting new things is Imbolc.

Summary

1. Celebrate.

Imbolc – Starting Anew

There are three spring festivals in Druidry because of the historical importance of spring to the farmer, but this is also in tune with our mood at the time. The first spring festival occurs about one-and-a-half months after Christmas, on February 2nd, and is called Imbolc or Candlemas in Christianity. This is a beautiful festival where we light candles in honour of the Goddess Brigid, a Celtic Goddess of poetry, healing and blacksmiths. They had varied accomplishments these Celtic deities! However, what it means is being aware of the growing light in our lives as the earth moves towards the sun and the days get longer. The reason this festival is dedicated to Brigid is because we are starting to wake up from our long winter somnolence now and beginning to feel like doing something creative, hence the poetry and blacksmithing. So I'm not asking you to get out and get the forge stoked up as I can readily understand that blacksmithing is not something all of us indulge in. Neither is poetry, some people love poetry and others hate it. It is also a fact that not all people can write it. In fact to be brutally honest there are some people who should never write poetry. However, Imbolc is a good time to get the creative juices flowing and start on something new, to be creative in whatever way suits you. If you haven't got a hobby, now would be a good time to start one.

Summary

1. Start something new.

The Spring Equinox – Go Out and Explore

After Imbolc comes the spring equinox, when day and night are in equal balance. In the Northern Hemisphere this is normally (unless you live in England!) a time when you can see visible signs of spring, i.e. mid-March with flowers appearing and the chance of some mild weather. Spring is when we start to feel happier and ready to be out and about again. So now is the time to shake off the winter sleep, put aside your new creative project that you have been working on and get outside and see the world again. Go out and see the crocuses and daffodils, marvel at the colours and the new green bursting out all around you (or probably struggle through the wind and rain, but this is living too). The important thing is to feel the enjoyment, the promise and, most importantly, the hope. The world is made new and all things are possible and this is true for you as well. Hope and joy are two elements missing from a lot of our post-industrial lifestyles and human beings are simple creatures and need these two feelings to thrive, so make sure you give yourself the opportunity to feel them.

This will set you up for the run into summer.

Summary

1. Get out and feel the hope.

Beltane – Fecundity

Spring is also the time when a young man's fancy turns to... Beltane! Most people have heard of Beltane, which occurs on or about the first of May. In our urban environment of Guildford we have the local Morris Dancers coming to the High Street and dancing (well, what a surprise!) and erecting their May Pole in the castle grounds. Depending on how you feel about Morris Dancing you would either love or hate this, but it does mark out the urban year and many local people turn out to watch regularly. The Barker hands out fertility cake (OK, a fruit cake stuck on the blade of a sword!) and they have a mischievous pantomime horse that surprises people by standing quietly behind them. All very silly really but symptomatic of how people feel at this time of the year. Many people know the descriptions in Thomas Hardy about couples in the bushes in rural England but this is hardly practical in an urban street (if we are to believe the media UK couples go abroad to do this!). Beltane is also about sex and sex is about creativity (literally), so whatever facet your creativity takes, indulge it at Beltane. Often by May it is sometimes warm and pleasant in the UK, so just sitting and revelling in the warmth is celebration enough.

One of the good things about Druidry is that it embraces all aspects of life; it acknowledges that we are not supermen or women and that we will do bad things as well as good. We are encouraged to note the bad things and try not to do them again but we do not dwell on them. Druidry also embraces sex as a natural part of life. This does not mean that Druids are always at it, in fact they might be indulging less than normal but we accept that it happens between consenting adults. It all comes back to personal responsibility which I said I would return to. In Druidry your morality is entirely up to you, no one is going to tell you how to live your life. As a flip side to this, the onus is on you to live your life in a genuine way and be true to your own code of morality and not be a moral butterfly constantly flitting from one code of behaviour to another.

Summary

1. Be creative.

Of course then we are on our way back to the summer solstice again and the cycle goes round. If you become aware of the passing seasons and year in this way you will feel more grounded and more a part of life rather than an outsider and this will help immensely. You will find yourself looking forward to some quiet rest as the days draw in and anticipating the joy of summer. When this happens you are living Druidry, it is that simple.

Chapter 5

Personal Responsibility

If you are a normal male, there is no need to run because I have used the 'R' word, I know that this sounds really offputting but it really isn't. Personal responsibility is about being true to yourself. If we all took responsibility for our actions then the world would instantly be a much better place. Of course the chances of this happening are pretty miniscule as we (if we are honest with ourselves) are a bit lazy and apt to overlook this or to try to get away with things by blaming others. Basically it is about 'walking your talk', if you say something try not to do the exact opposite. Let your behaviour show your moral code and be an example to others.

Walking Your Talk

This doesn't mean that we should all become high-flying moral philosophers but it does mean paying attention to the small things. If you object to litter and you see some then pick it up. Don't express your indignation and wait for someone else to come along to solve the problem. I read a nice letter in the CPRE (now called the Campaign to Protect Rural England) magazine about a group of older people who started a rambling group. If they encountered litter on their rambles they would pick it up. If they came to a car park and found litter outside someone's car, they would pick it up smiling all the time. In this non-confrontational way they managed to change people's attitudes. OK, this is just in one small area but it's a start.

The One Hundred Monkeys

Here is where I depart from New Age philosophy again. There is a story that is popular in New Age circles about the Hundred Monkeys, which was popularised in a book by Lyall Watson in the seventies. The story goes that in 1952 a group of Japanese scientists were observing a group of Japanese monkeys on the island of Koshima. The scientists were putting sweet potatoes in the sand on the beach and watching the reaction of the monkeys. One female monkey named Imo discovered that she liked the sweet potatoes better if they were washed in the sea, the salty taste of the washed potato being more to her liking. She taught the other monkeys and more started to wash their sweet potatoes until one hundred monkeys did it. Whereupon suddenly all the monkeys on the island and even those on neighbouring islands who had had no contact with the original group knew instinctively how to wash their sweet potatoes. It is a beautiful story and it has had a beautiful history. Many esoteric groups have taken this story as their inspiration and it was an icon of the anti-nuclear movement in the 1970s. The question is if humans behave the same, what is the hundredth monkey level for humans? How many converts do you need before suddenly everyone's behaviour is changed?

If you look at the original research papers nothing like the behaviour above is ever reported. Yes, sweet potato washing increases but the older adults never learnt to wash potatoes and even some of the young never learnt. There were some instances of monkeys on other islands washing potatoes but only a few. As I said it is a beautiful story and we would love to believe it but the truth is it never happened. There is no magical shift of consciousness observed at a certain proportion of the population, we are all responsible for our beliefs and behaviour and there will always be those who disagree with us. This should be no surprise because it is exactly how one finds the world and leads to a truly positive conclusion. YOU can make a difference.

Do What Thou Wilt

There is another area where I take issue with neo-pagans as well and that is in the misinterpretation of Crowley's 'Do what thou wilt, shall be the whole of the law'. This is often taken as licence to be as selfish as you like and become a hedonist. In fact it doesn't mean that, you won't be surprised that it means exactly what I said at the start of this rant (err... section). It means find out what is right and correct for you and then do that. You could end up living exactly the same life that you do now with this philosophy, but you would have actually chosen to live like that and that is fine. The more modern interpretation of this adage is 'Do what thou wilt, and it harm no one, shall be the whole of the law'. A very significant change of emphasis and more in keeping with what was originally intended.

Conspiracy Theories

This is the moment to talk about conspiracy theories. There are many people who believe that 'they' are responsible for a variety of things from alien visitations to global warfare. However, if you have ever worked in an office or been part of a group of some kind, e.g. a church or even Druid group (called grove in our terminology) then you will know that cooperation is a rare thing. Yes, people can get along for a short while before they fall to squabbling and disagreements. This normally arises because most people don't want the responsibility of being in charge and telling people what to do, so they think they are happy to coast but they aren't really. Most people actually think that they could do a lot better and resent being told what to do, even if they have actually let someone else get into that position of responsibility over them. The result of this is inevitable and the group soon disbands in bickering and argument.

This is what happens on the small scale, it takes no great leap of the imagination to see what is going to happen on the larger scale. Some conspiracy theorists would have it that we are being controlled by secret societies that have existed since the dawn of time. That is a very long time to keep cooperating and on a statistical basis the probability is almost negligible. Add to this that most people really enjoy blurting out secrets and you soon see that secret things won't last very long either. So do yourself a favour and reject conspiracy theories, be positive and realise that it is up to you, no-one has a vested interest (secret or otherwise) in seeing you fail and you can make a difference all by yourself.

Behavioural Assumptions

So examine what you do, do you really like or want to do all the things that you do or are there some things that are better left out? Are there things that you would dearly like to do and things that you could do less or drop to make space for others? In a rigorous magical/spiritual course you would also examine the assumptions that you live under and see if they are appropriate for you. For instance there are lots of behaviours that we carry out which are conditioned by society and we are mostly unaware of what these are but carry them out anyway. In essence these are the characteristics of a good citizen, like doing a good day's work for a good day's pay or being a consumer. However, these are the most difficult to deal with and are better left for the 'advanced' advanced course.

In many years of tutoring Druids I never cease to be

surprised at comments like, 'I never realised that I was hurting people by my promiscuous sexual behaviour, it was always their fault that we broke up and never mine'. Personal responsibility also covers sexual behaviour; the best adage is to ask yourself, 'Is what I am going to do going to hurt someone else?' If the answer is yes, then you know you have a choice. This adage applies to everything else that you do because I also find it amazing how many people seem to have no concept of how their actions and behaviour will look or feel to someone else. In the extreme cases, I have heard people say that 'my recollection is different'.

Of course everyone reads the situations that they are involved in differently. I am surprised that eye-witness accounts of events tally as often as they do! It is very instructive to ask your friends/partner how they perceived an event, you might be surprised! We naturally assume that how we perceive things is obviously how others do but this is often not the case and actually asking can clear up a great deal of misunderstandings and heartache later. However, there is such a thing as the absolute truth, something did actually happen and it is possible to extract this by examining the situation carefully.

Moral Evolution

I wish that I could give you the distilled wisdom of the ancient Druids on this point but I can't. For one reason they didn't write anything down and secondly the morality of the Bronze Age and Iron Age was somewhat different to now. This doesn't mean that Druidry is irrelevant to life today, however. If we look at the spiritual evolution of humanity then in the beginning humans were afraid. They were afraid of the wild animals, afraid of the weather, earthquakes, etc; and filled their world with a multitude of mostly uncaring Gods and Goddesses who were responsible for these phenomena and to whom they had to pray to placate. People were basically pawns in the hands of powers much greater than their own. As time went on, the vast number of these supernatural beings decreased until we eventually arrived at the twelve Gods and Goddesses of Ancient Greece, for instance.

The next evolution in Western thought was to move to the monotheistic revealed religions like Christianity. However, while Roman Catholicism wasn't conceived in this way, the way it came to be practised by the people didn't particularly stress responsibility. In the Catholic Church you are basically sinful and need to confess to a priest to get absolution. Another supernatural being called the Devil tempted you into bad ways, so it wasn't really your responsibility.

The big step with the rise of Protestantism was the internalisation of responsibility with the concept that God was watching you all the time and would shake His white locks sadly if you did something bad. You actually had to feel truly sorry yourself for Him to forgive you i.e. personal responsibility. The rise of Methodism in Victorian times added the Protestant work ethic to the mix, but in the process of industrialisation, humanity's connection with the natural world was broken. Hence the rise of neo-paganism where people are trying to reconnect to the natural world they have lost and there are many people who believe in a whole host of Gods and Goddesses again. However, this is coming full circle without evolving, we don't want to go back to those fear-filled days and lose the moral evolution we have struggled for. This is where Druidry comes in, we can keep the hard-won personal responsibility along with our need to reconnect to the natural world, everyone is a winner!

If you live your life with concern for others' feelings and extend them the same courtesy in choice of life that you give yourself then your life will be better and more fulfilling. Let's be honest here, don't you actually want people to like and respect you? If you don't please throw this book away as I can't help you.

Summary

1. Evaluate your code of existence.
2. Be true to it!

Chapter 6

Living a Longer Happier Life

There is some evidence that expressing our creativity, getting in tune with life and living in a way that is true to our own beliefs contributes to a long life. In a talk that I heard, war historian Max Arthur asked one of the surviving World War One veterans what he had done to live so long. Had he cut down on the bacon, etc. and the response was, 'Well, it's pretty good isn't it'. Not quite the answer one would have expected, basically if you feel good about your life you will live longer.

Obviously the veteran was comparing his situation to that of those who had lost their lives in the war and I would hope that many of us don't find ourselves in this position. Being happy with your life is key, as many of us know stories of people who have given up a job that dominated their lives and on retirement haven't known what to do with themselves. Quite soon they have departed this plane, so keeping an interest is vital.

Learning not to worry is also key. Science actually comes to our help here because scientists have recently proposed a theory that is called hormesis and this is the way to live a long life. Like most scientific theories it is actually pretty simple and obvious and is best expressed by the old adage that 'a little of what you fancy does you good'.

Hormesis

Hormesis states that if you stress your body in some small way then the body's repair mechanisms kick in and fix that problem. If it is a small problem the body's repair mechanisms also fix other things. So the essence of this is that if you challenge your body with repeated little stresses you actually improve your overall condition. So if you want the odd can of beer then that's great, it may actually do you good and if you feel like sitting in the sun for a while then it could also do you good. The key fact of this is the concept of a small stress, so if having a can of beer in the sunshine is good then 40 Player's Navy Cut and 20 pints of lager must be better. No! If you binge and repeatedly damage your system then you overcome your body's repair mechanisms and do permanent damage. So don't worry about the occasional indulgence, you could actually be doing yourself good and worrying about everything that is or might be harmful isn't helpful and could put you into a permanent state of stress.

Summary

1. Keep an interest in life.
2. A little of what you fancy does you good.

Chapter 7

Living Lightly on the Land

Druids are encouraged to live lightly on the land and what this means is to make your impact on the environment as little as you can. This doesn't mean that you should grow your hair, live in tent and join a peace group (although I do know some Druids who do). It means wake up and be aware of what you do. Most people these days accept that recycling of waste is a good thing and putting your recycling out on the appropriate day is one way in which you can achieve this. You can go further and buy recycled products, etc. The extent that you do this is really up to you (it's actually another example of the personal responsibility thing). Likewise many people use low energy light bulbs and energy efficient appliances.

Food and Waste

However, a major area of waste for most people is food. The amount of food that is thrown away in the UK alone is truly horrendous, so one easy way to live more lightly on the land is to eat less food or rather buy less food and actually eat it. Many people say that they don't have time to cook a proper meal in the evening. What do they have time for? The act of preparing and eating a meal with a partner or friend is one of the most relaxing things that you can do in the day. I'm not talking about Cordon Bleu or Michelin starred food here, just a simple nutritious meal. Most people can actually manage this and if you do it together it is a bonding activity too. OK, then you have to wash up and let's be honest here, no one is ever really going to enjoy doing the washing up but it is an opportunity to practise your living in the moment skills. If you pay attention whilst you are doing it, it passes relatively painlessly. Procrastinating and whingeing about what we have to do wastes a large amount of our time and if we actually got on and did it, we would find that it doesn't actually take that long.

Now we come to the thorny problem of what to eat. It is a fact that you cannot exist on this plane without consuming something and even plants are living creatures until you rip them from the earth. So you need to accept that something is going to die so that you can live. It is a fact of life and can't be got around. It is then your choice as to whether you are going to consume animals, fish or plants or some combination of them. If you view things this way it follows naturally that you shouldn't kill more than you can eat and you have achieved living lightly on the land.

Eating less also has important health benefits. I suffer from asthma myself and I had heard that many asthmatics are sensitive to certain foodstuffs, which can induce attacks. I haven't found this personally; what I have found is that eating too much affects my breathing and this in turn brings on my asthma. So the solution for me is simple, I stop eating before I am full and have been a great deal healthier as a consequence. Eating too much also educates your system to expect more and it is a downward spiral from there. In some weight watching schemes they educate people as to what a 'normal' plateful of food is and it is surprising how many people cannot judge what a sensible portion is. The positive side to this is that if you eat less, you can savour your food more and it is much more enjoyable (remember the aim is to live more fully in this world and actually experience your life).

When you get into your mid-forties, there is a lot of

evidence that your metabolism slows down and you therefore need less calories than you did when younger. If you keep eating the same amount then the result is inevitable...fatness. So a bit of common sense in your consumption in your middle years is very sensible.

Growing Your Own Food

Growing your own food has become extremely popular in recent years, fuelled no doubt by scares about pesticides, etc. If you have a small piece of land in your garden you too can grow your own. Even if you only have a windowsill you can grow your own herbs. In small pots on your windowsill you can grow for example chives, parsley or basil. There is a small caveat with parsley as folklore says that only a virtuous woman can grow parsley, so here's your chance to find out! There is also a caveat with basil in that if your house isn't warm enough it will wither and die very easily.

If you have a small area in your garden you can grow most of the vegetables that you eat regularly. The difficult one is tomatoes, as most people want to grow them forgetting that they really like quite warm, wind free conditions and these conditions aren't that common in the UK at least. If you want to start growing something start with potatoes as they will grow just about anywhere and the strong roots that they produce break up the soil nicely. They also act as their own anti-weed devices as the large foliage screens out the weeds from the sun. So if you grow potatoes first you will have nice soil for your next year's growing. In organic allotments crop rotation is practised with potatoes first, then beans (to put nitrogen in the soil), then the hungry brassicas and then back to the beginning again. This works very well.

This brings us nicely to allotments. Waiting lists for

allotments have increased exponentially in recent years. This is both a good and a bad thing. It is great that more people are interested in growing food but it is bad in that it adds to the pressure on those who have allotments. If you are unfortunate enough to have an allotment society in your area then the chances are that it is peopled by control freaks who are concerned with tidiness. I mean when have you ever seen a tidy farm? This attitude detracts from the enjoyment of getting out in the open and seeing things grow. Incidentally don't believe people who tell you that allotments can be managed in half an hour a week. It is true that the aim of an allotment is to keep an average family self-sufficient in vegetables. This amount of work naturally takes a great deal more than half an hour a week. When you add to this the need to trim the grass and edges to keep it tidy to please the allotment committee, then you are looking at a fairly hefty commitment in time and effort. Naturally if you do have the time it can be extremely enjoyable and satisfying and nothing beats the pleasure of eating fresh vegetables that you have grown and harvested yourself. In fact if you can manage to grow sweet corn, the taste is exceptional and completely unlike shop bought corn on the cob because when they are picked the sugar in them starts to turn into starch. So purists would say that you have to bring your pot of boiling water to the allotment to enjoy corn at its best. The ones you buy in supermarkets may have stood around for a while before you enjoy them.

Summary

1. Reduce your waste.
2. Eat sensibly.

Chapter 8

Expectations

Another aspect of living lightly on the land is expectations. It is a fact that our disappointments in life are proportional to our expectations. As a corollary of this if you expect nothing then you won't be disappointed. Of course none of us can live like this or would really want to, so we all have expectations. These are mostly things like a bigger car, bigger house, sexier partner or better job. Some of these are useful as they push us to succeed in life but as I said earlier they also lead to stress. So when you have reviewed your expectations as part of your personal responsibility check from the previous chapter then you also need to see if you still require them. Do you want a bigger house because your friends/family have one or is the size of house that you now have actually right for you?

Bear in mind that a bigger house means more cleaning, more bills, etc. Ask yourself if you can't make some small modifications to your current abode that will make it more acceptable. If you do want a bigger house because you want to keep up with the Joneses then you can always say that actually you choose to reduce your environmental impact and live lightly on the land by living in a smaller dwelling. You never know you might make them think too!

The same process should be applied to your current vehicle, is it actually what you want? Many ladies drive huge tanks around when the kids are small but actually yearn for a nippy runabout that is easy to park. Do you need a car at all, or two or three cars, which is the current trend? If you don't have several cars you might not need to concrete over your front garden and contribute to the flooding problem in the UK. If you don't concrete over your front garden you might plant some hedging which will give the sparrows somewhere to live and they might not still be an endangered species. You can watch them flit to and fro and listen to their friendly chirps which will help you to reconnect with nature and life. This is all achievable by one choice, choosing to live more lightly on the land.

Summary

1. Re-evaluate your expectations.

Chapter 9

Environmental Awareness

OK, so now we come to environmental awareness, yes, you guessed it the save the whales, tree-hugging proselytising that you were expecting from a Druid, and you are right many Druids are like that. However, there is no requirement to be like this, some people like direct action others prefer to express their environmental awareness by giving money to charity, etc.

I am amazed at the number of people who tell me how depressed they are, saying their friends never contact them and so on. If you ask them if they actually contact their friends themselves, normally the answer is no, they are passively waiting for someone to make them feel special. Unfortunately, like everything else in life this is up to you. I have noticed that if you move yourself to do something for someone else then you instantly feel better and you can break the depressive cycle. There is nothing to make you feel better about what you have than seeing someone who hasn't had or got your advantages. If you get involved in environmental causes, you are instantly a more interesting person and if you like group things you will have gained a number of new friends. If you are known as the local charity expert people will seek you out to ask you things.

In my department at work we have charity teas from time to time where people (often somebody's hard pressed mum) provide cakes which we buy by making a donation for a specific charity. We planted a whole copse of trees for the Woodland Trust in one event and everyone feels much better. Little things matter as I said before and if we all did something, how powerful that would be.

Summary

1. Do something for someone else.

Chapter 10

Medicine and Herbs

There is a tendency among New Agers to embrace alternative therapies and many of these are very beneficial, but like everything else there are lots of people waiting to take your money. Many Druids like to use herbs and get involved with herbal medicine.

Herbs and Cooking

This can be as simple as adding fresh or dried herbs to your cooking to add flavour and as a way of reducing the amount of salt that we take in. There is a theory that everyone in the Western world actually has higher blood pressure than naturally as a result of salt intake. Salt is a requirement in our diet as the sodium is used in nerve conduction, but it is added to a wide range of foodstuffs. To be fair in recent times manufacturers have become aware of this problem and have taken steps to reduce the amount of salt added to processed foods, for example.

Herbal Supplements and Medicine

Herbs can be taken further in a Western herbal or traditional Chinese medicine sense as a supplement or in some cases as a replacement for pharmaceuticals. Don't get me wrong, there is strong case for pharmaceuticals, antibiotics are a valuable tool for health and some of the anti-cancer drugs, etc. are extremely impressive but equally if we live a healthy lifestyle and take the appropriate supplements we can reduce our need for these valuable tools. In the case of antibiotics this will actually help as overuse can lead to bacteria becoming immune to them. Additionally, if you are generally healthy then you can fight off infection much more easily, so everyone benefits.

I am not a medical herbalist so the best way to find out about these is to ask one. Likewise there are many good qualified traditional Chinese medicine practitioners. Yet again, we come back to the 'C' word, it is a matter of personal choice as to whether you take herbs or not, but finding out about them is not only interesting but could actually aid your health.

With some of the more exotic techniques and remedies I feel that there is always the question of what is called in science 'the placebo effect'. What this means is that if you believe strongly enough that a certain medicine or technique will heal you then it probably will. There is currently no way that science can quantify the power of belief, and faith can certainly move mountains. So, many people report definite benefits from some techniques that I would describe as outlandish, but if it works for you then great.

The Psychology of Illness

In the beginning I talked about how our language can indicate and to a certain extent determine how we feel, this is also true in health or more properly in illness. I know of many people who put in long hours at work only to find that when they do get a holiday they are ill. The obvious solution is not to get yourself into that state to start with by taking sufficient breaks beforehand, but one of the main reasons why this happens is the attractiveness of illness. 'The attractiveness of illness?' I hear you query, 'is the fellow barking mad?, there is nothing attractive about illness at all.' Indeed I agree, being ill is not pleasant or is it? When we have a cold, we make loud barking noises commonly called coughing to warn people to keep their distance, our noses and eyes stream with the tears that we are shedding for ourselves, our throats are sore and we find it difficult to communicate, in fact we just want to be left alone, i.e. to have some 'me' time. This then is the basis of illness, we want some time to ourselves, to indulge ourselves, to be looked after as we feel we are not normally. This is all perfectly understandable, sometimes we just want to give up the daily struggle with commuting, the family, the in-laws, the mortgage, etc. After a few days' indulgence we feel like we can cope with it all again. Likewise with stomach upsets, we just can't stomach it any more. This is not to say that these are all imaginary problems and if we just pulled ourselves together we would be fine but it does indicate why some people 'go down' with whatever's going and others don't.

There is often a payoff for the sufferer in illness that, if we are honest with ourselves, we can see. This can be true in cases of chronic illness, where sufferers from these are expert at manipulating those around them. The detailed examination of this would be worth a whole book (and as you guessed there are several out there).

Note, I do not denigrate those struggling with really quite debilitating and sometimes life-threatening illnesses, these people are examples to us all. What I am talking about here is being aware of your needs before you need to resort to illness to get them.

Sometimes when an idea is in your head it seems to collect evidence as it proceeds and this is true in this case.

A recent publication of an article in the medical journal, The Lancet, about the effect of exposure to green environments on both the chances of surviving life threatening illnesses and the effect that green spaces make on the health of socially deprived groups, is particularly relevant. A green space is defined here as 'open undeveloped land with vegetation' and includes parks, recreation grounds and river corridors. In the first case access to green spaces has a positive effect on survival from a range of diseases ranging from circulatory disease to lung cancer. In the second case, even in the most socially deprived groups, the more the access to a green space the greater your longevity and the less the chance of dying from circulatory disease. There are lots of studies that support these findings and there are thought to be two main reasons for this. The first is that access to a green space gives you an opportunity to exercise and this is obviously beneficial in keeping you fit and healthy. The second reason is the psychological benefit of being in a green space and its effect on the reduction of stress. Hence from a psychological health perspective having the opportunity to get back in touch with nature could both reduce your stress levels and help you to live longer. There's a good argument in favour of Urban Druidry!

Summary

1. Try using herbs in your cooking to reduce salt consumption.
2. Can you find a role for herbal medicines in your life?
3. Get out in nature.

Part 2

The Advanced Stuff

What you have done, if you followed Part 1 is an Urban Bardic Course. Most modern Druid Orders are organised into three grades and these are Bards, Ovates and Druids (in fact OBOD is even called this). This reflects a semi historical division for which there is little actual evidence. Nevertheless, Bards are associated with creativity and the arts, Ovates with healing and divination and Druids with ritual, law and responsibility (to which we add these days service).

Bards

In order to benefit from a lot of Druid training it is important to free your imagination and this is what a Bardic course seeks to do. Of course as you have found, getting in touch with what is around you is a lot of fun too and Bardic courses are also about fun. In historical Druidry, Bards were trained to compose songs and poetry by lying down in the dark with a large stone on their chests. I have no doubt that this would encourage you to get on with the task quickly but these days this is no longer considered necessary! Another major aspect of historical Bardic training was the rote learning of material. As writing was somewhat of a secret art in Celtic times, the oral tradition was very important and Bards were the keepers of this oral history. Therefore Bards were required to learn by heart the songs, poems and stories of their culture as well as being able to recite genealogies, so that people knew where they stood in the history of the tribe.

There is little point in following this training these days, with the wealth of information available at the touch of a button, but there is value in memorising something. If you are of mature years then the act of memorising something, which is more difficult with age, helps to keep your mind fresh and alive. Also these days, young people reach for the internet instantly on being presented with a question. This can only lead to severe mental laziness, so there is value too in learning something by heart when you are young.

There is a serious side to Bardic courses too and this relates to the light body exercise. When you are meditating you can also access the light body. This concept has been known by many names in many mystical orders over time but the basic idea is always the same. The light body is considered causal to the physical body and not *vice versa*. It pervades the space that the physical body occupies and nourishes and heals it. Hence getting in touch with the light body regularly can improve your health.

The caveat however is related to the concept of chakras, for which there is not a simple Western substitute concept. Basically the chakras are a concept in Hindu metaphysics and are thought of as energy centres in your body, which are associated with the expression of thoughts and feelings, among other things.

Activating the light body serves to also activate your chakras, a little like throwing on a main switch. This has the function of bringing up your 'stuff', i.e. the psychic damage that you have done to your chakras through the act of living. One of the objects of Druidry is to become a whole person and that of necessity involves dealing with your 'stuff'. However, this is not to be approached lightly and requires the correct approach and lots of support. Therefore I am not going to go any further down this road and will just point you to a proper course (like the OBOD home learning course).

At this point I should also mention Awen again, this is the source of inspiration that Druids seek. To feel the flow of Awen in your life is to be truly alive and it is what drives us to create works of art or even write books! So to actively feel this force is a goal of Druidy. When Druids gather we often chant the Awen, where we make the word three syllables, i.e. ahh...ooohh...enn.

When you have a group of people chanting this, it is incredible and when the group chants this inside the circle in Stonehenge you can hear the stones ring. Incidentally this may actually be one of the reasons why Stonehenge looks like it does, with the stones slightly concave on the inside to reflect the sound waves. Of course most of Stonehenge is incomplete these days so one can only imagine the effect the chanting would have had when the circle was complete. If you want to know more about this I recommend reading *Stone Age Soundtracks* by Paul Devereux, which explains it far better than I can.

Therefore 'real' Druids try to chant the Awen every day to bring inspiration into our lives. This inspiration goes by many names throughout history, Rudyard Kipling famously called it his demon that inspired him to write but it has also been called a muse. OK, most of us aren't going to be inspired to write like Rudyard Kipling, but whatever you call the inspiration, it is what gives you a thrill and you know that it is what you must do. Naturally this inspiration can come to you anywhere, even in a big city, so is another reason why Urban Druidry works.

The third aspect of a Bardic course is creating a Bardic grove, which can be physical and/or internal. The word grove is heavily overused in Druidry, which can lead to confusion. In modern Druidry a grove is either a personal sanctuary, a physical clearing in a wood or forest or a group of Druids who celebrate together, lead by at least two fully fledged Druid-grade Druids.

In this case we will concentrate on the internal sanctuary. This version is particularly suited to Urban Druidry where you can create a safe space in your imagination. You can retreat to this space to find peace and tranquillity. A grove is a clearing in the forest surrounded by trees, so we imagine ourselves in this space with the trees surrounding us, the grass beneath our feet and the sky above. This space is normally circular because a circle has a definite edge and what is inside is clearly defined from what is outside. This is necessary to create the distinction in your mind and to allow you to feel separated from your concerns and secure in your space.

In Druidry we enter this space in our imaginations and just experience feeling safe, calm and free of distractions. Just as in meditation (which it is a form of) it doesn't have to be done for very long at one time, but the regular practise of it builds the feelings of calm and security over time and greatly helps your mental health. With all the distractions and annoyances of modern life, a place of sanctuary is a useful boon and if it is internal then you can take it anywhere and be in it anywhere. Additionally, as a calming technique this is really valuable. Naturally, there is a lot more to this as well, but this is just an introduction.

Ovates

The second stage of modern Druid training relates to the Ovate stage. While there is good historical evidence for Bards, there is little for Ovates, the closest being vates, the Latin word for a prophet. Prophecy is something that is viewed with suspicion in the modern world, but was a way of life in the ancient world, where nothing was done without first reading the omens. There are those that still live in this way these days but the majority of people would accept that we have free will and can live our lives in the way that we want. Therefore there is little use for prophecy in our lives apart from the vicarious thrill of reading your daily horoscope in the newspaper. The prophecy that modern Ovate courses concentrate on is imagining the future you.

As you can hardly have failed to notice we all carry a lot of baggage around in our lives and do things that we either don't want to do or that are forced on us by society or friends. The point of an Ovate course is to become aware of what we do, why we do it and whether we still need to do it. In this way it becomes possible to reimagine ourselves and change our behaviour. This process is the basis of a lot of mystical training in many traditions over the years and the approaches to it can be subtle ranging to catastrophic. The Druid way is gentle and accepting, we never force anything. This has the downside in that it can sometimes take a long time to achieve change but it is change that you personally can cope with. The observant amongst you will have noticed that I used the word reimagine above and this is the link to the reason for having the Bardic course first. You can only reimagine the new you if you can imagine something anyway, so firstly you need to free your imagination to be able to imagine the new you.

Whilst the concept of Ovate sounds quite simple when stated above, after many years of Ovate tutoring I can honestly say that this is the hardest part of the whole course. Many of us are stuck in our ways, are not very clear about our motivations, we do things that we know we shouldn't but still do them and are reluctant (for a variety of reasons) to change our ways. As a Druid tutor I am forbidden to interfere and I have lost count of the number of times I have heard what a tutee wants to do, thought privately 'don't do that' and had to stand back while they do. Several years later they will come back and say, 'I shouldn't have done that'. Again this Ovate process takes careful handling with a lot of support and is best done under the aegis of a properly designed course. There is a lot more to it that I'm not going to go into here, but eventually the student will pass through Ovate and arrive at Druid. This is something that is also unusual about Druidry, it is initiatory, i.e. you become a Bard and then learn how to be one, you become an Ovate and then learn how to be one and you become a Druid and then learn how to be one.

Druids

The historical Druids were attached to the staff of kings and chiefs and served as advisors, lawgivers, sometimes even peacemakers. They are also thought to have presided over sacrifices, some of which were human sacrifices, which were carried out by the Ovates. Things were very different in those days and clearly human sacrifice is frowned upon these days, so this is a role that modern Druids emphatically do not get involved in. A modern Druid grade course seeks to pull together the skills that have been learned in Bard and Ovate training to produce a fully functioning human being. As you have probably realised this is more involved than it sounds but paradoxically easier than the other two grades.

We add the concept of service to the role of the modern Druid. Once you get there what are you going to give back, i.e. what are you going to do for the Order, your fellow man/woman or society? Doing something for others is a great way to feel good, improve things around you and generally contribute to an upward trend in society rather than a downward spiral into selfishness and anarchy.

Many modern Druid-grade Druids run groves, which as mentioned before are groups of like-minded individuals that meet to celebrate the eightfold year and practise Druidry. I am not that familiar with Wicca, but a high-grade Wiccan can start their own coven, which is a similar concept except that you need two Druid-grade Druids to form a grove. It helps if these are male and female as we recognise balance and males and females have different and complementary things to contribute. Added to this in our group rituals there are words traditionally spoken by the female Druid and those traditionally spoken by the male. Although we recognise that a Druid of either sex can express both energies, it is simpler this way. Having said this, in our local grove, my female Druid colleague and myself often swap roles depending on who is doing what in the ceremony and to keep us on our toes. What I particularly enjoy is meeting with a bunch of Druids and laying down my posturing and position in society and just relaxing in the spirit of acceptance and just being me. This is a great way to unwind and revel in the joy of life... and did I mention the hugs!

Conclusion

So there you have it, it is really easy to follow this simple outline in order to live your life more fully and be more present in the here and now. To be honest, what else is there actually?

So if you make these simple changes to your life you will have become an Urban Druid without the necessity of buying a single white robe or even a false beard.

Of course if this piques your interest and you would actually like to learn more about Druidry, I have included a list of contacts at the end. There is of course no requirement to do this, the techniques outlined in the book work for everyone regardless of your spiritual or religious persuasion. There is also no requirement to do any of the techniques outlined in this book, but your life will be the poorer if you don't.

There is no magical technique that will change your life overnight because change requires effort to overcome inertia (or entropy if you are of a scientific bent). The nature of the universe is to resist change, so if you make small changes over time you will be able to sneak over this barrier without noticing it. All you have to do is keep at it, in a small way, until it becomes permanent. The key is to keep at it, we all start things enthusiastically and little by little we backslide until we are right back at the start. That is why this book concentrates on small changes that don't take a great deal of time, so that you can remember and do it until you have changed your lifestyle completely. In Buddhist retreats they ring a bell at regular intervals to remind you to focus on the present. Think of this book as a series of little (thankfully soundless) bells that act to remind you to stay with the change.

So good luck, enjoy your fuller, more exciting life and welcome to the growing ranks of the Urban Druids.

Further Reading

There are a variety of good websites and books for those who want to learn a bit more about what I have just briefly mentioned. Firstly the references from the text:

The Cloudspotter's Guide by Gavin Pretor-Pinney, 2006, Sceptre. ISBN: 978-0340895894.

RSPB Handbook of British Birds, 2010, http://shopping. rspb.org.uk/p/BOOKS/R0158.htm.

Urban Wildlife (Usbornes Spotters' Guide) by Diana Quick, 2006, Usborne Publishing Ltd. ISBN: 978-0746073643

The Woodland Trust, http://www.native-tree-shop.com/ swatch-books/leaf-swatch-book.

No, there isn't a guide to non-feathered bird spotting, shame on you!

Free Your Breath, Free Your Life: How Conscious Breathing Can Relieve Stress, Increase Vitality, and Help You Live More Fully by Dennis Lewis, 2004, Shambhala, ISBN: 978-1590301333.

The Book of Meditation: The Complete Guide to Modern Meditation by Patricia Carrington, 1998, Element Books, ISBN: 978-1862042360.

The Madness of Modern Families by Annie Ashworth and Meg Sanders, 2006, Hodder & Stoughton Ltd, ISBN: 978-0340923412.

The Campaign to Protect Rural England, http://www. cpre.org.uk/home.

Lifetide by Lyall Watson, 1987, Hodder&Stoughton Ltd, ISBN: 978-0340231197.

Last Post: The Final Word from our First World War Soldiers by Max Arthur, 2005, Weidenfeld and Nicholson, ISBN: 978-0297846444.

'When a little poison is good for you' by Mark Mattson and Edward Calabrese, New Scientist Magazine, 06 August 2008.

Cooking With Herbs & Spices: Easy, Low-Fat Flavor by Judy Gilliard, 1999, Adams Media Corporation, ISBN: 978-1580622196.

The Herbal Medicine Maker's Handbook: A Home Manual by James Green, 2000, Crossing Press, ISBN: 978-0895949905.

The Healing Power of Illness by Thorwald Dethlefsen and Dahlke Rudiger, 2002, Vega Books, ISBN: 978-1843330482.

'Effect of exposure to natural environment on health inequalities: an observational population study by Richard Mitchell and Frank Popham', The Lancet, 372, 1655-1660, 8th November 2008.

Stone Age Soundtracks by Paul Devereux, 2001, Vega Books, ISBN: 978-1843334477.

Secondly there are also many informative texts about Druidry, only a few of which are listed here:

A short description of the key beliefs of Druidry:
What Do Druids Believe? (What Do We Believe) by Philip Carr-Gomm, 2006, Granta Books, ISBN: 978-1862078642.
An account of a modern Druid's walk in the country:
The Druid Way by Philip Carr-Gomm, 2006, Thoth Publications, ISBN: 978-1870450621.
Modern Druidry with a focus on the Welsh folk tales of the Mabinogion:
The Path of Druidry: Walking the Ancient Green Way by Penny Billington, 2011, Llewellyn Publications, U.S. ISBN: 978-0738723464.
Modern Druidry from an Irish perspective:

The Druid's Primer by Luke Eastwood, John Hunt Publishing, 2012, ISBN: 978-1846947643.

A modestly named but very informative text:

Principles of – Druidry: The only introduction you'll ever need by Emma Restall-Orr, 1998, Thorsons, ISBN; 978-0722536742.

'Real' Druidry

There are a large number of Druid groups worldwide, the largest of which is the Order of Bards, Ovates and Druids, (OBOD) which is philosophical in bent and runs a home learning course. The website is: www.druidry.org

The British Druid Order, which devolved from OBOD and has a more shamanic bias also has a website: www.druidry.co.uk

ADF, An Draiocht Fein is the largest American Druid order: www.adf.org

The Council of British Druid Orders maintains a site, which in true Druid fashion OBOD is not currently a member of: www.cobdo.org.uk

The current (May 2013) members of CoBDO are given below:

Glastonbury Order (GOD)
Insular Order of Druids (IDO)
Universal Order (UDO)
Druids of the New Aeon
Bardic Order Group (BOG)
Loyal Arthurian Warband (LAW)
Dorset Order of Druids (The Dolmen Grove)
Iolo Morganwg Fellowship (IMF)
Cumbria Druid Order
Cotswold Order (COD)
Wandering Peace Poets(OWPP)
Phoenix Order of Druids
Druid Order of Tamaris (DOT)
Druids of Albion (DOA)
Albion Conclave
Druid Order of the Red Dragon

Moon Books invites you to begin or deepen your encounter with Paganism, in all its rich, creative, flourishing forms.